I0493241

21 Digital Marketing Ways to Advertise on a Shoestring Budget

By Devin Zellars

Note to the Reader

While the writers of this book have attempted sensible endeavors to guarantee the precision and convenience of the data contained in this book, the writer and distributer expect no obligation as for misfortune or harm brought on, or charged to be created, by any dependence on any data contained in this and repudiate all guarantees, communicated or suggested, as to the exactness or dependability of said data. The authors make no representations or guarantees as to the precision or culmination of the substance of this work and particularly repudiate all guarantees. The exhortation and techniques contained in this book may not be suitable for each circumstance. It is the finished obligation of the peruser to guarantee they are holding fast to all nearby local and national laws. This production is intended to give precise and definitive data as to the topic secured.

No part of this distribution might be duplicated, put away in a recovery framework, or transmitted in any structure or by any methods, electronic, mechanical, photocopied, recorded, filtered, or something else, aside from as allowed under U.S. copyright law, without the former composed authorization of the creator.

Contents

Marketing Ideas

Marketing Plan. Creating a marketing plan is one of the best strategies you can invest your time. By writing out a simple plan that outlines the vision for your business, objectives, strategies and a plan to accomplish your goals, you'll be way ahead of the 80% of business owners who don't invest the time to do this. Know Your Niche. This is another fundamental to business success. Take time to identify and reevaluate who your ideal target customer is and write it down. Is it narrow enough? Even though almost everyone could use your product or services, trying to market to *everybody* is a sure way to get your message across to *nobody*.' By having a narrow niche you'll be seen as an expert and will stand apart from the crowd.

Create a Great Logo. It is imperative that your small business has a logo that represents your company. When you choose your logo, it isn't as easy as closing your eyes and pointing your figure at a symbol or graphic. This logo represents you and your business, essentially your brand message. It encompasses your company's vision, mission, values and more. A good logo is what gets your business noticed and once your customers recognize your logo, that in turn will promote your services and turn to success.

Have a Great Audio Logo. an Audio Logo is how you verbally communicate your value proposition. Like your networking 1-minute introduction, you want it to position you apart from your competition and communicate your value in a compelling way. Remember to say who you work with, describe the problems you solve, share the benefits your clients get from your products or services and tell a client success story.

Voice Mail. Use your voice mail message to communicate a succinct, clever marketing message. Does your voice mail say…"I'm not here, beep." or does it say something more valuable about you and your business? Think of this as a free commercial – keep it short but use it to market your services, share an interesting and relevant tip, promote your tag line or simply drive traffic to your website.

Direct Outreach. One of the cheapest marketing strategies you can ever do is direct outreach. Get out there, talk to and meet people. Stop hiding in your office surfing the web. Make it a goal that you're going to pass out a hundred business cards. Whether you're pumping gas, in the shopping lineup at Safeway, at the fitness center, church or anywhere, find ways to talk to a hundred people this month. Count them off. Strike up conversations, find out what they do, use your Audio Logo and share information. Make it your goal to get out there!

Leverage Your Email Signature. Your email signature is valuable real estate. Not only should it have your name and contact information, but it should also promote your business. Here are a few ideas to spice up your email signature to build awareness, referrals, and potential prospects: • freebie to lure them to your blog or website • list top benefits your services or products provide • branded tag line • link to read or download interesting articles • link to a quiz • announce a new product or service launch • an invitation to an event.

Make an effort to have at least one link at the end of every email. Not only can you get visitors to your website, but you'll also build awareness of what you have to offer. The cost to you? Zero.

Promote with Your Vehicle. Use your vehicle as a moving billboard to get some added visibility and marketing. Whether you go all out and bear the expense of a full auto shrink wrap or just get an inexpensive vinyl sign on your door, your vehicle can bring you new customers. One of my client's gets 35% of his business from his vehicle signage. Signs of Success? Stand outside your business and take a critical look. What is your signage like? Does it represent your business brand well and entice customers to come in? Stop and think about how you can leverage your storefront. Is it easy to see what your business is? How about any specials, sales and promotions? Is your signage old, tattered or out of date? This is your customers' first impression – make it a good one.

Bulletin Boards. You'll find them in coffee shops, fitness centers, grocery stores, libraries, community centers, churches and more! Depending on your product or services and target customer, these are a great free way to get visibility and your message out in the community. Make sure your postcard or poster is well thought out, professionally branded and represents your business well. You'll want to have a special offer with clear instruction on how to find your physical or online location.

Networking. By far networking is one of the most inexpensive and effective marketing strategies to grow your business… but only if you approach it strategically. There are dozens of networking events and groups where you can meet, mingle and make connections. Attend the ones where you're likely to meet you target prospects or referral partners. Then come prepared with a smile, business cards and good conversational skills. Some basic guidelines:

• Don't be a wall flower – get out of your comfort zone and meet lots of people

• Meet new people instead of hanging out with people you already know

• Take on a host mentality

• Arrive early and stay late

• Don't sell

Follow up with people you meet.

Database…Database…Database… In the restaurant business there's the old saying "to be successful you need location…location…location!" Well in the service sector it's all about your Database. This is your key list of prospects, clients, and contacts. Focus on growing your database, adding to it as you expand your contacts. Treat your database like gold because it's your business community and main vehicle to communicate your marketing messages. Don't toss all those business cards you gather into a drawer, use CRM (client relations manager) software to track and communicate with your contacts. There are many free online versions – just do a Google search for "free CRM systems" and check them out.

Leverage the Season. Tap into a whole calendar of special days every day of the year and use them in your marketing. Yes, there are the ones we all know about like Valentine's Day, Thanksgiving and Mother's Day, but did you know there a plethora of celebrations you've never heard of? Find ones that tie into your business to create some unique marketing opportunities. Here are some to get you thinking - World Kindness Day, International Youth Day, Asthma Day, Wear a Hat Day, International Women's Week, World Sustainable Energy Day.

Get on the Phone. When was the last time you just called contacts from your database to connect and offer help? This is a great habit to get into. Make a point of either spending X amount of time or calling X number of contacts every day or week for the sole purpose of connecting. Remember when you call it's not a sales pitch – be genuine, find out what's new, ask who you can introduce to them or how you can help.

Business Cards. They come with two sides so use them both! Printing the back of your card will cost next to nothing. Some ways to leverage this bonus space:

• A more complete list of services

• Testimonial from a client

• Invitation for a complimentary consultation

• A link to an article, video or audio recording targeted to your ideal prospect. The new technology out now is that you can imprint a barcode on your business card so that people with smart phones and the barcode app can link to a website quickly and effortlessly.

• Top tips that are in alignment to what you do

• Link to a free special report or ebook

• Useful information

• Quote

• Special offer or promotion

Become a Master at Follow up. If you want to get better results from your marketing, you need to crank up your follow up. Often we don't need more new contacts; we just need to follow up with the contacts we've already made. Don't miss out on opportunities – schedule time after every networking event you attend just for following up with all your new contacts. Send them an email, note or call for a more personal touch.

Door Prizes. Bring a door prize to every networking event or business function you attend to offer to the host. Most will love it and you'll gain added visibility and recognition. If you're lucky, you may get to stand up and give your 15-second infomercial, just because you brought a bottle of wine, gift basket or a Starbucks card. It's a great way to contribute and stand out. Leverage your gift by including your business card and make sure to get the name of the winner so you can follow up and make a connection.

Special Promotions. Special promotions are an excellent way to revitalize your marketing and create a buzz. Here are a few ideas:

• Put something on sale

• Offer a buy-one-get-one free deal

• Have a special bonus or gift with purchase

• Tell-a-friend special pricing

• Send out coupons or offer specially priced gift certificates

Volunteer. Volunteering is a great way to position you –and get visibility in the process. To make it work to your benefit you need to volunteer for the right cause, for example in a place where you're likely to find prospects or potential referral partners. Good options might be Chamber of Commerce events or Charity golf tournaments. Or you could join an association with a cause you're passionate about. You'll develop valuable relationships, contribute – and get exposure.

Be Neighborly. Do businesses in your neighborhood or building know who you are and what you do? Go knock on the doors of other people in your building and introduce yourself. Find out about them and who their ideal target customers are – can you send them a referral? Share information about yourself and your business, you may be surprised at the result.

Special Events. Another way to get extra exposure is by staging a special event. Whether it's a grand opening, reopening, and tours of your facility or the launching of a new product or service. You could also stage a high-profile focus group, sponsor a discussion or host an event on your subject of expertise. All these ideas will give you exposure and bring you more prospects. Map out a solid plan to get the word out first.

Article. Write a signature article that addresses common problems your target customers experience and some ideas on how to overcome them. Now, it's not a sales pitch but you will showcase your expertise and position yourself as an expert. Use this article as a giveaway on your website or blog, in your email signature or networking follow ups. If you're more of a speaker than a writer, download Audacity free recording software, put on a headset, and record an informational talk. Get it transcribed and presto! You have a signature article (and audio).

And the Winner Is…. Host a high profile contest. Get a variety of businesses to donate high value prizes in exchange for the exposure. And then have the contestants do something that will be a bit of a challenge to maintain the interest of the press. Make winning the contest a big deal that people want to hear about. And of course, they'll be hearing about YOU all the while.

Build a Power Team. This is a BNI (Business Network International) concept that anyone can use. Look for successful non-competing professionals who service the same ideal target customers you do. Then make some outreach contacts to introduce yourself and invite them for coffee to see if there's a connection. Say to them, "I think some of my customers can use your services and I bet some of yours could use mine. Let's connect and see if we can help each other." Continue to build a small group of 4 – 6 professionals and then meet regularly to share leads, introductions and work on joint ventures together.

Referral Partners. A Referral Partner is anyone who recommends your services or products and consistently gives you quality referrals and introductions to qualified prospects. This marketing strategy is a powerful one that will bring you more clients with a lower overall expense and time invested. Prospects that come to you by way of Referral Partners are pre-qualified, which makes it much easier to convert them into customers. In fact, many of them literally arrive on your doorstep ready to buy. Your Referral Partners need to understand what you do, who you do it for, what you deliver and what problems you solve. They need to have a full knowledge of what your business is all about before they can successfully refer the right type of people to you. But how do you get Referral Partners? Check out MoreReferralsForYou.com.

Showcase Your Expertise by Speaking. Speaking is an awesome way to position yourself as an expert and gain visibility in the marketplace. If you hold your own seminars you incur the room cost and marketing expense to get people to attend. Some low cost venues worth checking out are community centers or libraries. An alternative to your own events is approaching associations to get booked as a guest speaker. Start by creating a few signature presentations that are relevant to your target customers and then contact associations you feel are a good fit. As a guest presenter there's no cost – you just need to show up and present. Make sure you find a way to capture contacts and have a call to action or next steps for the audience to engage your services.

Collaborate with Competitors. Stop competing with your competitors. Instead, find ways to collaborate. Successful people may have more business than they can handle at one time; projects that are too big or too small, or not ideal to what they do that you can subcontract with. Look for competitors to collaborate with – ones that you align with but don't compete head to head. You'd be amazed at how much business goes back and forth. So, collaborate!

Co-market. Look for opportunities to co-market with aligning businesses. This is where you join forces and share marketing dollars allowing you to book bigger advertisements to get more visibility and a bigger bang for your buck. Look for other successful services your target customers buy just before or after yours. Some ideas: A tire shop and a car wash; a dog trainer and a dog groomer; a realtor and a painter. The combinations are endless.

Seek to Add Value. If you want to attract more clients, you'll have to stand out from the crowd. And if you do stand out, you'll also get to be more memorable. Here's a way to differentiate yourself from just about anyone else: Most people tend to think about what they can get. So why not focus on how you can give instead? Think about how you can add value to something you offer, or how you can make a contribution to something you're involved in. By adding extra value you'll be an irresistible client magnet.

Get Testimonials and Case Studies. Nothing sells better than an endorsement from a past customer. One enthusiastic customer is equal to three sales people. So go through your client lists and start asking for testimonials. Generally, people want to give you a testimonial – but often they don't know how to write them. There's an easy way around this: offer to write it for them by first doing a quick interview with your client, record it or write furiously – you want to capture a few phrases that are exactly what they say. Then you write it and send it to them for review. They can make corrections, tweak it or even add to it. If you're a little shy about your virtues; they might pump it up a little bit more. Keep in mind that these are mini-marketing messages. For greater impact, try to quantify or 'dollarize' your clients' results and target a specific outcome to showcase different strengths of your services. That way you'll get an interesting range of testimonials or case studies. And finally, don't forget to express your thanks and gratitude to your customer.

Ask for Referrals. Do you have a strategy in place to consistently get referrals from your current clients? Often we assume that if we do good work for our clients they'll refer us. It's nice to believe that, and it can happen, but it will happen more often if you have a proactive approach. Develop a system to stay top of mind and consistently asking your clients for referrals. Make it easy for them. Start asking for referrals; make it a regular part of your communications and you'll be surprised with your results.

Make Connections. In this day of overflowing email inboxes, a physical card really stands out. Get into a routine to send out a few cards each week, and you'll generate a huge amount of goodwill. Thank, praise, acknowledge, appreciate or just say you're thinking of them. You don't even have to physically send the card if you don't want. There's a terrific service called SendOutCards.com where at the click of your mouse you can have a real card mailed out with your customized sentiment.

Contact a COI, Think about what centers of influence (COI) your target prospects know. Some obvious ones are the executive director from a chamber or board of trade or a trade association that you belong to and so does all your ideal target customers. Consider anyone who is well positioned in the business community. These are people that you want to befriend. Invite them for lunch, or if you don't have the budget, invite them for coffee. Get known by them. Because they know lots of people, they could refer or connect you. They first need to know you, like you, and trust you. Make a list of who you want to connect with and put it in your marketing plan this coming month to have a coffee date with one COI. It's a great no cost way (except for the cost of a cup of coffee) to get visibility and connected.

Pull Off a Publicity Stunt. If you want a lot of press, you'll need to give them something to write about or feature on the news. A good publicity stunt can do that. It doesn't have to be too crazy either – just creative. Think of some unique ways to get your name in the news – just make sure that it's legal, ethical, and that you're not going to be embarrassed or ashamed by it. Teleseminars. Presenting a teleseminar is an excellent free or inexpensive way to connect with your clients and prospects and generate new leads. It positions you as an expert at a fraction of the cost of holding a live seminar. And if you're nervous about public speaking no one will know or see you reading your notes! There are several free services like FreeConferenceCall.com where you can sign up for your dedicated bridge line. Then pick a topic that's of interest to your database, create a great title and content and promote it to your list. Email your database and invite other people through social media, business directories, discussion boards and forums.

Leverage Your Suppliers. Are your suppliers doing business with you? Do they even know what your business is? Some suppliers may not potentially be a target prospect, but they are in contact with dozens or hundreds of people that could be. If so, they'll make great referral partners. Here's a short list of suppliers that could be customers or send you referrals: Your accountant, attorney, plumber, electrician, graphic designer, daycare provider, house cleaner, gardener, mechanic, realtor, friends, family, your minister, priest, rabbi, dentist, doctor, spa, hairdresser, dog groomer, beauty consultant, any multi-level marketing product, health and wellness products, marriage counselor, coach, personal trainer, a financial adviser, and any other people you buy services from.

There are lots of opportunities - start by connecting and sharing what you do and who you'd like an introduction to. On the flip side, who can you refer to them?

Trade Shows. Now, you're probably thinking, "Oh, they cost a lot of money." They do if you buy the booth, but you can attend a Trade Show for free, or for a very low door price. Go as an attendee early in the morning when there's hardly anyone around and talk to exhibitors you feel would be good prospects or referral partners. Connect, exchange business cards, do a follow up, and you might have a hot prospect. As great conversation starter you might say, "Gosh, I was going to get a booth here but didn't book in time, how's the Trade Show been for you?" Remember – don't sell, just connect.

Newsletter or Ezine One of the best ways to build a relationship with your database, to keep you and your business on top of their minds, and to be seen as an expertise is to send out a weekly or biweekly newsletter or ezine. Make sure that your articles add value and are on topics of interest to your readers. Self-promote sparingly. If you find writing difficult use articles from your referral partners or download from article sites like EzineArticles.com. Using a low cost online emailing system like ConstantContact.com makes design, set up and distribution a breeze and they also provide reader statistics.

Reconnect with Past Clients. Don't forget about past clients – they can be great advocates for you. They used your services once and believing they were happy; they probably know other people they could refer to you. Even if a client left you to go to a competitor, forgive them, let it go. You might be surprised, sometimes they move to a competitor, but when the honeymoon is over and they're not as happy as they thought they'd be, they could come back to you. Make a plan to contact X number of past clients every week.

Survey Your Database. Are you up to date with the issues, concerns, needs or problems your prospects and clients have? A survey is great way to position yourself as someone who cares. The information you gather will get you into the mindset of your target customers and is invaluable for future product and service development and your marketing communications. Use a free online tool like SurveyMonkey.com.

Invest in a Great Head Shot. Leverage your social networking with a great head shot. You'll get a lot of mileage out of your investment because it will appear everywhere. You can place it on your blog, your Twitter profile, your Facebook page, and any other social media sites that allow photos. In addition, you'll include it in the profile section of all the article directories and business directories where you are a member. Having a consistent photo builds recognition.

Start a blog. If you don't have a blog yet, now's the time to get started. Yes, even if you have a website. Why? Because blogs are dynamic. They build community and give you the opportunity to create a personal connection with your prospective and current customers. In fact, it's a perfect way to mix the personal with the professional. You get to tell them about your newest products and services and also share some personal information. That makes the blog interesting, fun to read, and it helps your readers bond with you.

Article Marketing. Build a massive online presence by writing articles. Publishing your articles in online directories will position you as an expert bringing you a great deal of visibility and credibility. This is one of the easiest ways to drive traffic to your website −and it's free. Your articles need to be interesting and provide useful information. At the end of each article include a 'resource box' or bio that will lure people to your site, blog, or products. This means that all those articles will be like an 'agent' working on your behalf bringing you online visitors.

Use Article Directories. Here's how to start creating your army of article agents: Sign up as an author at the premier article directory - EzineArticles.com. You'll be taking advantage of one of the most powerful free online marketing tools. EzineArticles gets millions of visitors each month, so why not get your fair share? Even better, they have a high page rank, and their articles score very well on

Google. So if you write articles optimized for your special buying keywords some of your articles will be found on Google.

Write Lots of Articles. The more articles you write the more exposure and opportunities you have to get traffic to your websites, sales pages, blogs, squeeze pages, or anywhere else you want. Not only is it free, but all those articles will continue to work on your behalf for months and even years. More articles also improve your expert status giving you additional visibility and extra clout. Target writing and submitting at least one article every week.

Spread Your Articles Around. To get even more mileage out of your articles post them to several directories. Some good ones are: • buzzle.com • goarticles.com • searchwarp.com • articledashboard.com • articlealley.com • selfgrowth.com. Why go to the trouble? Because different article directories have different audiences. So while one article may get just a lukewarm response at ezinearticles.com it could do very well at another directory, and vice versa. You'll never know until you experiment. Either way, the net effect is more exposure and more visitors to your website.

Blog for Google Love. There's another reason why blogging qualifies as cheap advertising: Google loves blogs, and if you set yours up right and post regularly, Google will love yours too and reward you with great search engine positions. And that in turn means…visitors! Yes, that's how people will find you.

Use Keywords. Good keywords are at the heart of getting better ranking and getting found on Google. You need to strike a balance between aiming for keywords that many people are looking for and keywords you actually have a chance to be found for. That's not always easy, but a good keyword tool, including Google's keyword tool, will help. You might also try to get a good keyword tutorial.

Start Bookmarking. Social bookmarking sites are another tool to help you get the word out about your website, your blog, and your articles. They are communities of people who share articles they find interesting by "bookmarking" them, so that others can enjoy them as well. Check out a few social bookmarking sites - the most popular ones that you might want to start with are del.icio.us, digg, reddit, stumble upon, technorati, and propeller.

Join as many as you like (or feel that you can keep track of) and after writing an article or posting a blog post that you're really proud of bookmark your work. Remember, this is about building community –and too much self-promotion won't make you very popular. To avoid being seen as a moocher or spammer, be sure to bookmark other people's work as well.

Post on Business Directories. Get found by people looking for what you offer by joining business directories like HotFrog.com. There are dozens of business directories for a variety of niches. Find free ones that fit for your business and create a listing. Directories help you get found and can bring you new business, both by people who are searching for information in those directories, and from Google.

Discover Online Press Release Sites, You probably know that you can use press releases to try to get newspaper to write articles about you. But did you know that there are many free or inexpensive online press release sites too? Many free press release sites simply publish your press release online –and send it to other sites who may publish it as well. Of the low-cost ones, my favorite is WebWire.com – it generates quite a lot of visibility.

What can an online press release site do for you?

• They publish your press release, so people searching those press release sites may find yours too.

• Since many press release sites have a high Google ranking, people will also find you on Google especially if your press release is optimized with good keywords.

• All of the press releases linking back to your website make the search engines rank your website higher.

Join Forums. Joining a discussion forum is another great way to make new connections in cyberspace. Find relevant discussion forums in your niche by typing the name of your niche and "forum" into Google's search box. For best results, join ones that are active with new daily posts. This is a great way to build community and visibility with prospects. As a bonus, you can add a link to your website in your signature – and information about your business in your profile, so anyone who finds your comments helpful will be able to contact you.

Build Connections with Social Media. The advent of social media has changed small business marketing. It's no longer just about people putting up websites and others visiting those websites. The internet has become interactive, and many connections are made through social media. The biggest players are Facebook, Twitter and LinkedIn which should definitely be on your must-do list. Take time to create a profile on each of them and get involved. Consistency is important so schedule 30 minutes a day to maintain your social media presence.

Viral Marketing. How would you like to have others do your marketing for you? You can…with "viral marketing." The goal is to create a highly sought after product, special report or information on something that a lot of people would want that will get passed on from one person to another – just like the in the hot potato game. Then sprinkle links to your site(s), products, and services throughout that report (especially at the end), turn it into a PDF file, and give it away. You should also encourage people to pass it on to their friends. If the information is good enough, they will do just that.

Create an Easy Low-Cost Video for Your Website (and YouTube). Using a video on your website is a great way to build greater connections and create a sticky website that people stay on longer. Often, when we think about video, we think it might cost thousands of dollars. That's no longer the case. In fact, video has to be neither expensive nor complicated; all you need nowadays is your smart phone. And then give a few tips or explain a concept and invite people to have a look at something on your website. Keep the video short – around 2 minutes. Remember to post it on YouTube.

Video Creation for the Camera Shy. What if you're shy or otherwise uncomfortable with public speaking especially in front of the camera? Let a friend help by interviewing you. It's much easier (and fun) to answer questions and have a conversation about what you do and the result your clients get than stare into a camera. You can create a whole series of videos in an hour. They'll probably be better too since the energy of the interaction will come across to the audience. And that's important. After all, the purpose of doing videos is helping people connect. Other Types of Videos If you really don't want to be on camera, you have other options. You can create PowerPoint videos or mind map videos. No fancy equipment is needed for either of them. You probably already have PowerPoint, and you can get Free Mind mapping software at freemind.sourceforge.net.

Educate Everywhere You Go. Have lots of articles and information about how you help people, but not as a sales pitch. Instead share an abundance of ideas, answers, tips and "how-to's." Some people worry and say, "If I give out all the answers, I won't be hired." This is limiting thinking. In today's internet age, sharing information is key to positioning yourself as an expert, being attractive and getting prospects to come to you. So always seek to find opportunities to provide lots of information.

Repurpose Your Content. Any time you create content make sure to reuse and repurpose it. A teleseminar recording can become several articles, a special report or an eBook. A series of articles can become series, YouTube videos, an eBook, blog posts or articles and so on.

A Workhorse Website. Is your website just a flashy electronic brochure or does it work for you? At the very least you need to have a simple website but it can be much more than that. Start building community by having a Blog on the home page. But if you really want your website to earn its keep, create a free product like an ebook, top tips, special report or audio that's attractive to your ideal prospect. Position this free offer on your home page where visitors can request this valuable information.

Social Media

Facebook. We have to include this as our number one way to advertise inexpensively. Sure, there are other inexpensive ways out there, but this is the current wave. Ride it while it's popular.

How it works: Create ads based on your business goals. First of all you want to be clear as to what your business goal is. You want to get the best possible response from your advertisement. For example, let's say you're a travel agent and you want to sell a wine country tour package. You determine that your audience would be within the demographics of the ages between 28 years old through 60 years old. It wouldn't behoove you as a small business owner to spend money on a generic audience. You would be wasting your money if your advertisement went to people under the age of 21 since they won't be drinking wine. You can also narrow your intended audience by choosing the traits that best fit what you are selling. For the wine tour seller, they would probably want to advertise by location since they may have more sales if they advertised to more people in the vicinity rather than states away. Facebook makes it even easier because they provide tips for writing your ad and choosing the best photos, and it provides analysis, *i.e.*, how many people saw your ad, how people responded, etc.

How much does it cost? You create a budget and that determines when and how the ad gets shown. You can pay a specific amount per day or per campaign. It can be as little as $5.00. Facebook makes it easy to go back in and adjust your budget at any time.

Self-Advertising. When we say self-advertising, we mean what can you do yourself to promote your business. With Facebook, you can do this by creating a fanpage. This is very simple to do and worth the initial set-up effort. When you create your fanpage on Facebook, remember, this is the professional side of you, not your personal side of you. Your fans do want to see endless pictures of your food or your dogs or your vacation pictures (especially if you are gloating on how much money you made so you deserved the vacation). A cute puppy picture is okay once in a while, just don't overdo it. Your fanpage is for one purpose: to get customers, to keep them engaged and to sell your services. Don't embarrass yourself by posting nonprofessional material. This could cause your fans to leave your page. And remember, advertising by word-of-mouth is too effective to ignore.

Twitter. Here is another trending venue that is easy to use and provides a large audience. As a small business owner, you should already be on Twitter. Twitter can be an engaging and very interactive social media tool, but if you don't use it correctly, you lose. Twitter is meant to be an exchange of information and sharing. I tweet and you share my tweet; you tweet and I'll share your tweet. The mentality of sharing is what will get you far. If you only advertise yourself and your business and sell your product 24-7 without engaging with others, people are going to become frustrated and most likely ditch you. When you promote others and offer courtesy and manners, then the same will be done to you. As a small business owner, you need to be likeable because if people don't like you, how will you sell anything? Remember, the bottom line is to make money.

How it works: Twitter ads are designed by tailored campaigns. Analytical tools are available for easy tracking so that you can tweak it if it's not working. Twitter advertising can campaign to the groups you want to reach so that you can connect with the right people. Again, like Facebook ads described above, it doesn't make sense to advertise to groups that won't be beneficial.

How much does it cost? Just like Facebook, for Twitter advertising, you set the budget. You only pay when users respond to your promoted tweet. You are in complete control. That should be music to a small owner's ears!

Self-Advertising. As we mentioned above, "twitting" isn't all about you. It is a careful calculating give-and-take with others where we retweet their posts and they reciprocate. For a passive self-promotion of your services or business, you can *pin a tweet* to your twitter profile page. Pinning a tweet to your profile is akin to that important one-minute pitch because it is the first thing people see when they go to your profile. Your pinned tweet should be an attention-grabber with a call to action. We call it passive because people who view your profile will see it first and most likely retweet it; you don't have to do anything once you pin it. You can leave it pinned to your profile until you decide to substitute another tweet. This is well worth it.

Website. To some, this is so obvious that they are surprised that it's in this list. You would be surprised at how many small business owners still don't have a website. "We have enough customers," "We don't have the time to create one," "It's too time-consuming and expensive." It is imperative that a small business owner have a website. Let's take the first excuse, "We have enough customers." You may now, but what about in the future? What if several customers leave for different reasons? There are plenty of surveys and studies done telling us how much it costs to acquire a customer. And, it is well-known that it takes a while for a customer to trust you and your services - well over a year, even two. So you can't afford not to say you have enough customers - it's never enough. "We don't have time to create one." There are many web-building sites online now that it's crazy to say this. The templates available are colorful, interactive and so easy to use. You can build a website very easy for free using templates and you'll but up and running within a day. "It's too time-consuming and expensive." It's time consuming to NOT have a website. A website can be interactive and informative. It can draw customers. It will build you and your services or product. It can sell for you. You can't do and be all of that. With a website optimizing SEO (search engine optimization) you can sell to the world.

Pinterest. Pinterest is a great new social channel to advertise. This social media giant has 176 million users so something must be right. These users are active and love to share, so it is a great place to promote your business. The more colorful your promotion, the more likely the users will "pin" or promote your posts. Take advantage of this social craze.

YouTube. YouTube is a global video-sharing website. We've all heard of it or have watched a video from YouTube. It's not just for watching music videos anymore - it is so much more. From cooking, to home improvement, to demonstrations, you name it, you can view it on YouTube. You can make your own video and upload it to YouTube to promote your business. There are so many idea that you can take up: provide an info-commercial about your services, you can have someone interview you, you can demonstration how to do something. The ideas are endless. And when you upload to YouTube, you can also upload your YouTube video to your website, Facebook fanpage and even pin it to your twitter page. Social media at its best!

LinkedIn. LinkedIn is another easy self-service pay per click service. If your business is looking for a strictly professional audience, LinkedIn is worth a try. You can select a target audience by specifying criteria such as age, gender, company name, geography, etc. There are several ways you can advertise on LinkedIn and all may or may not work for you. So depending on your marketing strategy, you will need to determine what will work. Because LinkedIn ads may be slightly higher than other social media sites, you would want to monitor the analytics to see if you want to continue with the advertising campaign or edit it for better exposure.

Vine. Vine is a video sharing service where users can share video clips that are six seconds long and continuous looping. Vine's app can be shared on Facebook and Twitter but competes with Instagram and Mobli. How can you advertise with Vine? It can be used a promotional tool and you can post a reveal, say, a new product that your business just produced. It's simplistic and gets the point across - in six seconds.

Instagram. With more than 400 million users, Instagram might just work for you and your company. With Instagram, you can be creative as you want to be. The users love quality content. You can select from photo ads, video ads and "carousel" ads (people can swipe to see additional images with a call to action button). Facebook bought Instagram in 2012 so advertising with Instagram would be a win-win.

Google Places

Google Places is a straightforward service from Google to help small business make themselves visible and searchable on the internet by people from a particular locality they cater to. Google Places is free and allows businesses to put themselves on the web with little effort, which makes the service and excellent marketing option for small business owners.

Google Places is the local Yellow Pages – With the internet at hand, there are very few people who still search for a service using the traditional Yellow Pages directories. So besides being listed in the traditional Yellow Pages, businesses should also consider getting listed in online directories and in Google Places, especially if the business caters to a local audience. The advantage of using Google Places is that all the relevant information about your business is available and can be accessed by your potential customers through the internet, even when you don't have a website. So if you are a small business owner and haven't had the time to create a website or have time to maintain it, Google Places is the viable solution for you.

Improved search engine page ranking – Google Places focuses on local searches, which means that the competition for a local business o Google Places would be restricted to the other business only within the locality and not the entire region, city or state. This means that there are better chances of your business being at the top of the search engine page results for your category and location.

For example, a search with key terms – 'Italian restaurants in Somerset, NJ" would only get results for Italian restaurants within the region and not the entire state of New Jersey. So, the possibility of your Italian restaurant being found is much better in Google Places.

Your business is easily found on Google Maps – Another advantage of getting listed in Google Places is that your business would also be marked in Google Maps, giving the exact location of your business to a potential customer. When you allow your business listing to be found through relevant keywords used in Google Maps, which also works on mobile phones, customers on the move, who are looking for your service, would be able to find you without much hassle.

Cost-effective local marketing – The obvious reason for a small business to use Google Places is that it is a free service. Spending huge amounts of money on billboards, television, radio or print ads is not a practical option for small businesses. Google Places on the other hand allows small businesses to advertise to their potential customers in a given locality and costs much lesser than traditional advertising options.

Making the best use of Google Places

Now that you know about the benefits of Google Places, here are a few tips on how you can make the best use of this service.

Use keywords – Use relevant keywords properly to create an impressive product or service description that appeals to the customers. But avoid overusing or stuffing of keywords, otherwise your search engine page ranking could go down drastically.

Add Images and videos – Business owners listed in Google Places are allowed to add up to 10 images and 5 videos for free. Make the best use of this and upload images of your business establishment, so that it becomes much easier for customers to find and identify you.

A Google Places page for every location – If your business has different branches at different locations, make sure that each branch has a separate Google Places page with the location's address and phone number. In case you have just one branch but offer services in different locations, you can create a single page and list down the areas in it.

Encourage reviews – Ask your pleased customers to review and rate your services on Google Places. The higher your ratings, the more number of customers you can get. Try to get as many reviews as possible, but only from genuine sources. However, avoid having too many just for ranking as this can cause Google to push your listing down.

How to Advertise on Google for Free

In order to set up your Google My Business free listing, you'll need the following information at hand:

A brief description of your business.

Your phone number, address, website, hours of operation, and any other contact info you want to advertise.

A logo or image that represents your business (for example, a picture of your office, store, or restaurant).

To set up a Google My Business listing, follow these simple steps...

Step 1: Set Up Your Account

Visit http://www.google.com/business. To set up your business on Google My Business, click the 'Get on Google' button below the text, "Get your business on Google for free."

Get-on-google-1

Keep in mind that your Google My Business account will be connected to your Google account. First, search to see if your listing already exists. Keep in mind that you can edit a current listing at any time to display new information about your business -- you just have to access the Google account used to create the listing, or request access from the owner. If you don't yet have a listing, create one from scratch by clicking 'Add your business.'

Claim-business

Step 2: Provide Your Business' Location Information

Once you click 'Add your business,' Google will initially prompt you to provide the location information for your business as well as your business' main phone number and category.

Add-your-business

If you don't have a brick-and-mortar storefront (for example, if you're an online business that sells goods and services to customers at their locations), check the box at the bottom of the form to list your company as a service area business on Google. This will enable you to set up service areas based on either the zip codes or cities you serve, or within a given area around your location. Then, when people search for a business similar to your listing, your business will appear on a map within this specified range.

If your business serves only certain cities or areas within a city, you can choose the first option and pick only the areas you serve. This option can be helpful for companies that are only able to serve a certain area (such as a pizza delivery company) or operate in a very niche market (like a jet ski company on a beach).

Service-areas

Step 3: Confirm Your Business & Agree to Terms of Service

Before you complete your business' full listing (which Google allows you to manage as a Google+ page), you'll need to confirm that the information you've entered up until this point is accurate, as well as agree to the Google My Business Terms of Service.

Confirm-business

Step 4: Verify Your Business

Before Google can make your listing visible to the public, it needs to verify that your business is legitimate. This helps Google avoid fake listings and advertisements. Google will mail you a postcard in 1-2 weeks with verification information and next steps. As an alternative, you can verify your business via phone. (Here's how.)

You can skip this verification step for now if you want, but ultimately, you'll need to verify your business if you want your free Google advertisement to be live.

Verify-business

Step 5: Complete Your Business' Listing Information

As I mentioned earlier, Google now uses the information from your business' Google+ Page to power its Google My Business listings in search results, so the next step is to start editing your Google+ Page. Click the red 'Edit' button at the top of your page to get started.

Mike-fake-bakery-google-plus-page

Then, start filling out your business' details. Here is a full look at the type of information you can include:

Edit-business-profile-1

Some of these details will automatically populate from the information you previously provided in Step 2. You'll also want to add your website, hours of operation, the profile photo for your business (for example, your logo or a picture of your storefront), and an "introduction." Your introduction should be a brief description of your business. Think of it as a tagline. Be sure to add keywords you want to get found for in search, and try to keep your introduction short and sweet so it doesn't get cut off in Google My Business search results.

Step 6: Optimize Your Business' Google+ Page

While the information you provided above is all Google needs to include your business among its Google My Business listings in search results, it's wise to take some extra time to optimize your business' Google+ Page -- especially considering your Google My Business listing in search results will include a link to your business' Google+ Page. To optimize your Google+ Page, click on the drop-down arrow at the top left next to 'My Business' and select 'Google+ Page.'

Optimize-google+-page

What to Optimize on Your Google+ Page:

Cover Photo: Upload a high-quality, compelling image as your page's cover photo. This image should be representative of your business as well as eye-catching and visually appealing. Download a pre-sized template to create your Google+ cover photo here.

Your Story: Think of this as a mini 'About Us' page, and use it draws your visitors in with a clear and concise explanation of your business. Elaborate on your business' description and the products/services you provide, and include any keywords you're hoping to get found for in search.

Links: Add any additional links you want visitors to check out. In addition to your business' website, do you have a blog you want to point people to? An event you're trying to drive registrations for? A particular landing page you're promoting?

Photos & Videos: To make your page more interesting to visitors, add photos and videos of your business, the products/services you offer, or anything else related to your company. If you own a restaurant or another business that lends itself to a virtual tour, you can hire a Google-certified photographer to create a virtual tour for your business that can be featured on your page as well.

Status Updates, Events, and Polls: Keep your business page fresh by regularly sharing status updates, posting about events your business hosts, and engaging with your followers by publishing polls.

Reviews: Respond to reviews left about your business.

Settings: Manage your page's settings via the left-hand drop-down navigation. Here, you can set up notifications, edit your page's managers, etc.

Chamber of Commerce

A **chamber of commerce** (or **board of trade**) is a form of business network, for example, a local organization of businesses whose goal is to further the interests of businesses. Business owners in towns and cities form these local societies to advocate on behalf of the business community. Local businesses are members, and they elect a board of directors or executive council to set policy for the chamber. The board or council then hires a President, CEO or Executive Director, plus staffing appropriate to size, to run the organization.

The first chamber of commerce was founded in 1599 in Marseille, France. Another official chamber of commerce would follow 65 years later, probably in Bruges, then part of the Spanish Netherlands.

The world's oldest English-speaking chamber of commerce, in New York City, dates from 1768. The oldest known existing chamber in the English-speaking world with continuous records, the Glasgow Chamber of Commerce, was founded in 1783. However, Hull Chamber of Commerce is the UK's oldest, followed by those of Leeds and of Belfast in Northern Ireland.

As a non-governmental institution, a chamber of commerce has no direct role in the writing and passage of laws and regulations that affect businesses. It may however, lobby in an attempt to get laws passed that are favorable to businesses. They also work closely with a number of other youth organizations in the country about the value and role of business in our society today.

Membership in an individual chamber can range from a few dozen to well over 800,000, as is the case with the Paris Île-de-France

Regional Chamber of Commerce and Industry. Some chamber organizations in China report even larger membership numbers. Chambers of commerce can range in scope from individual neighborhoods within a city or town up to an international chamber of commerce.

In the United States, chambers do not operate in the same manner as the Better Business Bureau in that, while the BBB has the authority to bind its members under a formal operation doctrine (and, thus, can remove them if complaints arise regarding their services), the local chamber membership is either voluntary or required by law. In addition, Chambers represent the interests of businesses, while the BBB represents both the interests of businesses and the general public. Some Chambers are partially funded by local government, others are non-profit, and some are a combination of the two. Chambers of commerce also can include economic development corporations or groups (though the latter can sometimes be a formal branch of a local government, the groups work together and may in some cases share office facilities) as well as tourism and visitor bureaus.

Some chambers have joined state, national (such as the United States Chamber of Commerce and the British Chambers of Commerce) and even international bodies (such as Eurochambres, the International Chamber of Commerce (ICC), Worldchambers). Currently, there are about 13,000 chambers registered in the official Worldchambers Network registry, and the chamber of commerce network is the largest business network globally. This network is informal, with each local chamber incorporated and operating separately, rather than as a chapter of a national or state chamber.

How to use a chamber of commerce to help grow your business

For centuries, businesses have reaped the benefits of joining chambers of commerce. But beyond the myriad of networking opportunities, there are many ways a chamber can help your business grow and thrive.

According to Vicky Hawke, executive director of Northern Ohio Area Chambers of Commerce (NOACC), networking is the No. 1 reason businesses join a chamber. "For the small cost of a chamber membership, businesses have access to other businesspeople in the community," she says, adding that chambers also address and serve the needs of the business community through education and advocacy issues.

The dollars-and-cents savings that go along with a chamber membership is NOACC's sweet spot. Founded in 1995, NOACC currently offers benefits to almost 35,000 employer groups through the members of 133 chambers of commerce in northern Ohio.

The largest independent chamber association in the United States, NOACC was created to attract and retain members in local chambers of commerce by offering significant discounts and rates on benefits businesses want.

Local chambers join NOACC and pass savings on to their members who can take advantage of the programs and effectively improve their businesses' bottom line. "People don't join the chamber of commerce to help the chamber; they join the chamber of commerce to help their business. It's not a contribution; it's an investment in their business," Hawke says.

NOACC's member benefits include group health insurance and group life and disability insurance with Anthem Blue Cross and Blue Shield, workers' compensation group rating programs, credit card processing and payroll processing services with Heartland

Payment Systems, freight delivery and employee-wellness programs.

The caveat to reeling in the savings? Members have to take the first step in receiving the benefits. "Neither the chamber nor the vendor is spending a lot of time in trying to sell them anything," says Hawke. "They have to actually go looking for it and they have to ask 'Is there a discount because of my chamber membership?' or 'How do I get this discount?' It's like any other membership buying group — you must take advantage of the savings."

The organization negotiates with vendors to get group discounts for their members. For example, companies that opt for health insurance coverage with Anthem Blue Cross and Blue Shield can receive a 3 percent discount for groups between two and 50. If they also enroll in Anthem life insurance, that discount can be as much as 5 percent. In the case of workers' compensation premiums, NOACC has saved companies up to 90 percent of their premiums. "We save our members millions of dollars every year between the various benefits we offer," says Hawke.

AnswerNet

Get the word out to customers and prospects and free up your time and resources by asking AnswerNet to handle your Outbound Telemarketing. Connect with your customers and clients with a complete range of outbound telemarketing services.

Whether business to consumer or business to business, AnswerNet's outbound telemarketing services get results.

Customized, Attentive Customer Acquisitions Using Outbound Telemarketing

AnswerNet's goal is to turn each outbound telemarketing contact into sales and results. We select, assign, train, supervise and monitor top-performing agents. Ask us to customize scripts for different market segments using appeals that will get results.

Tap into our product expertise and knowledge to gain the strongest results for your outbound telemarketing program. AnswerNet can connect you to contact centers and staff who have had the most experience and success at handling similar outbound telemarketing projects in your industry vertical or regional market.

Get the most outbound telemarketing leads and sales at the lowest cost. We employ predictive dialing software on large-volume campaigns that enable high agent productivity.

Effective Lead Qualification Using Outbound Telemarketing

Determine your true sales prospects by asking AnswerNet to qualify leads for your sales team. We can warm transfer hot leads. We can also close lesser-value outbound telemarketing sales. Your sales professionals are free to pursue the higher-value deals and build relationships with top buyers and prospects.

Making...and Ensuring Appointments Using Outbound Telemarketing

Ask AnswerNet to take care of appointment setting so that your sales teams can focus on getting those handshakes and signatures. Let our outbound telemarketing agents qualify leads, see whether prospects are interested and set up the times with our online appointment scheduling program. We can also send out reminder emails or outbound voice messages to confirm appointments.

Hot prospects on the lines? AnswerNet's outbound agents can patch in your sales staff to complete the deals. Customers/prospects wish to change or cancel appointments? We can supply toll-free numbers or email addresses.

Quality List Management for Your Outbound Telemarketing Campaigns

Sound accurate, lists are key to effective outbound telemarketing campaigns. Our list scrubbing services eliminate duplicate names and phone numbers. We can test lists to help you identify ones that will be most productive.

Through our partners AnswerNet scrubs names against Do Not Call lists. That way we reach customers and prospects that are potentially receptive to your offers. We help you meet all regulatory requirements to ensure program compliance.

Caring for Customers by Using Outbound Telemarketing Services

Outbound telemarketing is a powerful customer care tool. Let AnswerNet contact your customers to ensure they are enjoying your product or service and to see if they have any questions, concerns or suggestions. Ask our outbound agents to notify customers about hot deals keyed to their interests or about critical information like software bugs that show that you are looking out for them.

When customers are on the line is a perfect opportunity for cross-selling/up-selling telemarketing targeted offers. AnswerNet's outbound agents are trained to know the right moment when to turn outbound service calls into outbound telemarketing calls.

A Consultative Approach for Your Outbound Telemarketing Campaigns

AnswerNet cares about the success of your outbound telemarketing campaigns. We take a consultative approach in campaign design and management. Project managers meet with you throughout each step of your outbound telemarketing program to assess results and, if necessary, make adjustments.

Flexible Outbound Telemarketing Pricing

Outbound telemarketing entails risks. AnswerNet has low minimums, flexible pilot programs and customized pricing methods. We can work with you to make your outbound telemarketing program a success.

Capturing Live Leads From Events

So, let's look at a step by step process to capture live leads from events. For one thing, what should you do with all those business cards you collect? You could manually enter the details from the cards into your email system such as MailChimp etc., which would be a bit tedious but is better than doing nothing with them. Or you can use a scanning app such as Card Munch (details hooked up with LinkedIn) or Instant Customer (captures details and adds to your email program).

Remember, if you are at a live event, you already have a targeted audience in front of you. They are already interested in the area for which the expo is targeted so it is up to you to ensure that you effectively capture the leads. Here are some suggestions;

Don't allow people to just walk past your booth without giving them something! Many booth-holders are seen sitting behind the desk on their phones or looking disinterested. Engage with your audience!

Make sure you grab their details; use the 'ethical bribe' to get their name and email address. This could be a competition or free giveaway.

Capture their details either the old-fashioned way (pen and paper) or use technology. For example, you could set up an SMS service to collect name, email and phone number. You could also put a QR code on your booth or cards which takes people to your opt-in page once they scan it. Bequrious.com is a good site to set this up.

If you are speaking on stage, you could get people to text to a number to get your slides or enter for a giveaway. This is a very fast way of capturing many leads.

Capture leads by directing them to a landing page on your website for a giveaway etc.

Have a fish-bowl to collect business cards. Use an app such as Card Munch to scan the card for you and process the information straight to your LinkedIn account. Instant Customer will also put the details into your email data base.

The key to successfully capturing as many leads as possible at these events is to make it as easy as possible for people to engage with you. Go prepared and have the technology set up in an easy-to-follow way. Another tip is if you are collecting info by having people fill out forms; get your staff to fill the forms out to ensure that they are legible.

Email Campaigns

Salesgenie makes it easy to send professional-looking, effective email marketing campaigns to a targeted list of prospects. Simply use our Email Campaign Builder online or let our email marketing experts take care of all the details for you.

Tracking the performance of your email campaigns is imperative to future email campaign success. Below, we've listed several tips to keep in mind as you create and send an email to your targeted lists. Don't forget that our experts at Salesgenie can help you handle the details with email marketing.

Acquiring your customers via email campaigns is a marketing science that continues to evolve. Because of this, several teams within Salesgenie have collaborated in an effort to provide you with the means necessary to make your email campaigns a success. This section pertains to tracking the performance of your email. While best practices continue to evolve, these helpful suggestions will point any marketer in the right direction.

Before You Send

Subject Line Testing

Salesgenie can perform a subject line audit, which will identify any problems before a subject line is used.

Pre-Flight Report

Salesgenie can run an advertiser's email through a series of checks to identify problems prior to launching the email. Examples include a URL Blacklist Check (link checker), Cloudmark Check (testing the sender's address reputation) and Pivotal Veracity and Return Path Reporting (how your email looks across browsers and phones). These are all standard pre-send checks done at Salesgenie.

We highly suggest that every sender run these checks before any sizeable deployment. It has saved many email campaigns from disaster, and may help you too. At a minimum, running at least one email campaign through our pre-flight check will help you understand where your strengths and weaknesses are as an email marketer. You can then use what you learn to improve all your future campaigns.

Performance Tracking – Helpful Hints

Subject Line Testing

Each method of response you provide should have a tracking method in place. This is because once you know how well a particular email offer is working; it can and should transform your marketing strategy. With strong tracking, and the flexibility to respond to it, a good email campaign can take your marketing strategy to the next level.

Track Back

People often make purchases through a shopping portal at a later date. It's important to match this activity back and credit the campaign for this purchase.

Viral Marketing

Include a coupon or discount code that can be shared and used by anyone. Your recipient may not be in the market for your offer but could know a friend who is.

Target the Right Audience

Segment your audience based on specific sales criteria, including:

Type of Business including whether they are public or private

Companies within a specific ZIP code

Office size or square footage

Sales Volume

Referrals Techniques

Referrals are among the top ways sellers get leads and new business, but many struggle with generating them consistently.

Be referable. To make referral marketing a proactive part of your lead generation activities, you need to actually be referable. Ensure that you deliver what you promise, when you promise. Your clients need to be able to speak to the value you provide.

Don't rely on accidental referrals. It's important to get clear on who you want to attract as clients and how your network can help you get referrals to those clients.

Don't wait for the pipeline to dry up. Put a sales referral process into place now to drive high quality referrals consistently so that you're not left scrambling when the pipeline stops flowing.

Here are 15 ways to get more sales referrals in no particular order:

1. **Create a referral program with complementary providers to exchange referrals.** Be sure you only include providers in this network that you'd be comfortable recommending to your best client or best friend.
2. **Recognize and thank your referral sources.** This could be with a simple phone call, email, or even better, a handwritten note. The important thing is to express your appreciation. You'll also encourage additional referrals this way.
3. **If you have clients who don't refer, create another way for them to recommend you** (e.g., case study, testimonial). I once worked for a large organization that prohibited written testimonials and discouraged referrals; however, I was able to provide recommendations by phone for vendors with which I worked. Two vendors I worked

with took advantage of this opportunity and closed several deals by having select high-value prospects speak with me.

4. **Make sure your current clients know about all the products and services you offer and how you help** so they can either refer within their company or to others they know. Too often sellers assume their clients know more about them than they do. If you're a market research firm and a client uses only your online survey research services, for example, make sure they know about your intercept interview service or focus group capabilities.

5. **Add a link to a form on your website for referral submissions.**

6. **Be remarkable; remind clients why your company is special.** Give them something (good) to talk about.

7. **Inspire confidence.** It's risky referring someone—what if it's not successful? You can inspire confidence in your referral sources by letting them know that 80% (or whatever) of your business comes from repeat customers.

8. **Offer a referral commission.**

9. **Provide valuable content your referral sources can share with their network**—an invitation to a breakfast or lunch seminar or webinar on an industry topic, research briefs, an article about a regulatory change or industry trend, etc. Make it something special for them to share.

10. **Treat the vendors and suppliers with which you do business as partners.** Make sure they're aware of who and how you help.

11. **Update your LinkedIn profile** and stay engaged with your contacts regularly.

12. **Create a list of buyers you want to work with.** Check out their LinkedIn profiles to see whether you're connected in any way. If so, reach out to them via your network—whether it's an individual, a company, or a group.

13. **Treat your clients as partners, too.** Let them know you view them as a strategic partner, and tell them you hope they'll do the same with you. Create formal channels to share referrals.

14. **Give a referral. It's one of the best ways to get one in return.**

15. **Ask for referrals**. You'll get a lot more referrals if you ask for them. As you're completing a project with a client, simply ask if they know anyone who would benefit from something similar.

This is just a start. Let these suggestions jump-start your own idea generation. Create a sales referral process that works for your ideal clients and your networks.

Be referable. Focus on your ideal clients. Tap into your networks in a proactive way. By putting a referral system into place now, you are more likely to receive lead-boosting referrals throughout the year.

Lead Pages

As of today, that's all it takes to publish any Leadpage you create to your own website—no matter where it's hosted—after some quick initial setup.

This has been a top customer request for some time, so we're extremely excited to introduce our newest feature: domain mapping.

What does that mean?

First, let's back up a little. You've always been able to publish the landing pages you build in Leadpages in a variety of places: Leadpages' own super-fast servers, your WordPress site, your Facebook page (as a custom tab), or another server. Before now, that last option required exporting your landing page as an HTML file and then uploading it to your own server. Not terribly difficult, true, but not as simple as it could be.

Now, it really is that simple. In fact, it's the simplest way we've seen to publish landing pages to an external site.

What Is Domain Mapping?

Domain mapping allows you to quickly and easily map pages you create in Leadpages to domains you've purchased from a domain registrar (such as Bluehost, GoDaddy, 1&1, Namecheap, or Network Solutions).

For instance, let's say your Leadpages subdomain—that is, the word or phrase that appears at the beginning of every landing page you publish to our servers—is "stonebrookagency," and your main business site is stonebrookagency.com. Suppose you use Leadpages to create event pages and would like to make a webinar registration page to add to your site.

Leadpages Looks (and Feels) Different These Days. Here's Why.

It's all about you.

In fact, it always has been. Before Leadpages was Leadpages, it was a blog where founder Clay Collins occasionally posted videos dissecting landing pages. Eventually, in response to reader requests, he began releasing landing page templates. And as that audience tested the templates, provided feedback, and began asking for more, Leadpages grew into a company.

As of last week, the public face of that company looks a little bit different. You've probably noticed it if you've visited this blog, or signed into your Leadpages account: new look, new logo, new layouts, new overall feel.

Which Marketing Tools Are Right for Your Franchise? Look for Local Power and Centralized Control

Which marketing tools are right for your franchise?

Marketing for any large organization can get complicated, but it becomes exponentially more complex when that organization is a franchise.

That's due to one unavoidable factor: the franchisee/franchisor dynamic.

If you're involved with a franchise, you probably do have some system in place. In most cases, the franchisor is primarily responsible for promoting the brand nationally to drive franchise expansion. Meanwhile, the franchisees are responsible for local marketing efforts to get customers in the door.

The problem? Franchisees are rarely marketing experts. And even if they do have a talent for marketing, they almost never have a dedicated marketing staff to help them carry out campaigns.

That means local marketing efforts for franchises are often lacking: hastily executed, underdeveloped, or off brand. And because the brand is the core of any national franchise organization, brand consistency is paramount. The challenge many franchisors face is how to enable local franchise marketing without jeopardizing the integrity of the brand.

Before I joined Leadpages, I spent nearly a decade working for marketing agencies with franchise clients including Applebee's, Red Robin, Fastsigns, and Carquest Auto Parts (among others). I learned a lot about what does and doesn't work in franchise marketing, and ultimately I've concluded that there's only one overarching solution.

In the ever-changing world of digital marketing, at least one thing remains true: staying in touch with your email list on a regular basis is one of the best ways to build relationships. And relationships with your subscribers attract new subscribers, while turning subscribers into fans, fans into customers, and customers into evangelists for your company.

Sending a newsletter every week or two is standard practice for most marketers. If you're a blogger, you might even notify subscribers about every post.

It's a good start. But if you want to make the most of that email list you're working so hard to cultivate, a one-dimensional email marketing strategy like this isn't enough.

You can't just send out newsletters and expect that those subscribers will turn into paying customers (or even that they'll necessarily stay on your list).

In this post, I'll be sharing 17 kinds of emails that can help you get more out of your email marketing investment and your content in general, whether you're a blogger or anyone else who publishes content online. You'll find real-world examples of companies that are doing this well—sometimes delightfully well.

Last month, we released a huge new product development: a drag-and-drop landing page builder. Though it's still in early-access mode, we've been floored by both the response we've gotten from our members and—already—by the innovative pages they've built with it.

If you haven't had a chance to explore the new landing page builder, what you might not realize is that it's not just a drag-and-drop replacement for our existing landing page templates (which you can still use, by the way).

You can also do some pretty neat things you haven't been able to do with Leadpages before. Some are fundamental to the platform, some are cool perks, and some just make your marketing run a little smoother.

In every case, the drag-and-drop builder's features have been strongly influenced by requests from Leadpages users. Spend half an hour with our product team and you'll realize just how strongly: even after laying out the product roadmap, they're continually adjusting priorities and rollout schedules to deliver the things our customers tell us they need most.

Because of that, I won't be sharing exact timelines in this post—but I do want to give you a preview of some additional exciting developments coming down the line. Read on for 18 things you can do in Leadpages' drag-and-drop page builder right now, and 14 more that we're working on rolling out in the months to come.

The simple answer is: I had an awful case of blank page syndrome. I started and restarted; wrote and deleted. I broke focus and diverted my attention to other tasks that felt more pressing ... Like trying to curate the perfect mood playlist on Spotify that I was certain would make the words flow from my fingertips!

We all know that writing good copy for our businesses is important—but that doesn't necessarily make it any easier. The truth is: if you want your landing page to really work—if you want better results and more conversions—your landing page copy has to be good.

Not perfect. Not incredible. Not even great. It just needs to be good.

download landing page copy creative brief button

Good copy creates clarity in a world of short attention spans. It positions any business owner as an intelligent expert, and it helps your prospects know exactly what you have to offer, and then tells them how to go seize it.

It seems like anytime I get deep in conversation with a coworker at Leadpages, I end up learning something totally unexpected about them.

Like that they had a whole other career (or two) before doing what they do now. Or they've developed extraordinarily deep expertise in a different industry through consulting. Or they're using the marketing knowledge they've developed at Leadpages to help a family member get a business off the ground.

No matter how different the paths that took these people to Leadpages, one thing always becomes clear in these conversations: they're united in their endless curiosity and drive to figure out how Leadpages can help business owners in their area of interest generate more leads and grow faster.

The Build My Business series lets them explore that question by creating start-to-finish digital marketing campaigns for a fictional (but plausible) business of their choice. In each Build My Business post, an in-house expert or hobbyist chooses a business, a goal, and a digital-marketing-driven way to get there.

There's just one thing you might have missed, even if you've read some of these posts. Many of the marketing tactics inside don't just work for the business model being considered. They have the potential to make digital marketing a lot easier for a wide variety of businesses. Today, I'm taking a look at some of the coolest and most widely applicable ways we've found to make the path between site visitor and lead—or lead and customer—much shorter.

If you think of every eventual customer's story as a journey to conversion, these are the little workarounds that shave a couple miles off that journey.

To see how these tactics fit into a larger marketing strategy, you'll want to download our Build My Business Mega-Pack, which includes things like campaign diagrams, landing page templates, and resource sheets for the campaigns referenced in this post. Get the free collection here:

bmb roundup button Which of these 8 ideas could get leads into your database and customers through your door a little faster?

1. Shorten the Path from … Coupon Clipper to Customer

The shortcut: An effortless virtual coupon sequence

What you need to steal it: A service-based business, a LeadPages account, and an online appointment booking system

Here at Leadpages, we're constantly running tests behind the scenes to make our landing pages—and yours—more and more effective at converting visitors into leads.

Today—April 1, 2016—we're excited to announce a major discovery. After extensive A/B testing and user studies, we've found that, while there are many things you can do to make your landing page incrementally more effective, there's just one guaranteed way to ensure a higher conversion rate.

Video Submission Software Programs

You may have heard of video submission software programs, and may be wondering "What is Traffic Geyser?" And how can it help you in your business. I've been using Traffic Geyser for a couple of years now, and I've been looking for a Traffic Geyser alternative almost the entire time! Why? Well, because it's kind of expensive but to be honest I haven't found a legitimate Traffic Geyser alternative that will do what I want like Traffic Geyser does when it comes to video submission software.

Traffic Geyser is one of the best video submission software programs available, and it's very simple to use compared to a so-called Traffic Geyser alternative.

WHAT DOES TRAFFIC GEYSER DO?

In this article I'm going to show you how Traffic Geyser works for video submission, and how it can help you with SEO for your videos. Let's get started with the topic of "What is Traffic Geyser?" and how it can help you with video marketing.

IS THERE A TRAFFIC GEYSER ALTERNATIVE?

As I've mentioned I've tried to find a Traffic Geyser alternative but I just can't seem to find one that does what Traffic Geyser does as easy as it does it. Some of the Traffic Geyser alternatives are as follows:

Magic Submitter – Magic Submitter is a great piece of software, but it can be very complicated to set up. If you don't know spining syntax, or complicated video submission forms, don't even think about using it. I never got it to work very well for video which is my strength.

Content Buzz – Content Buzz looks pretty nice to be honest, and doesn't look that complicated. I haven't used it, so I'd love some feedback on this service if anyone has it.

Pixel Pipe – Pixel Pipe is software that does video submissions, but I don't know that much about it.

OneLoad.com – One Load used to be Tube Mogul, and you can't really do anything commercial here unless you pay $75 a month. They submit to good video sites, but no article sites or bookmark sites like Traffic Geyser.

MY VERDICT ON TRAFFIC GEYSER

I really like the service for what it does for me. I manage several blogs with Traffic Geyser and submit content to one portal for 15 article sites as well. I use excerpts for articles and it does a great job for me for SEO on my Videos, and supports my SEO efforts for my blog content as well. I'm getting back links to my videos, and multiple back links to my blog posts by posting the URL into Traffic Geyser.

I use this in conjunction with TribePro and between the two of them, I get a ton of traffic to my blog, and more views than I would otherwise without using Traffic Geyser.

I load my video one time as you can see in the videos on this page, and it submits them out to over 50 locations typically including over 15 video sites. I recommend you do your homework on what works for you, but for me I'm a faithful Traffic Geyser user!

traffic-geyser-video-marketing

Get a $1 Trial, and some GREAT Training Videos!

I strongly recommend signing up for the $1 trial to Traffic Geyser to simply get the Free Training they offer. It's THAT good! It's what really helped me the most when I finally figured out how to market with video.

The bigger problem with the private video hosting systems is that, for businesses to take full advantage of the marketing power of online video, **they need far more than just an online video hosting solution**. That's why so many single-purpose video applications have been introduced.

Here is a list of the single-purpose applications for online video that **aren't addressed by the private video hosting solutions** (with a sampling of some of the companies offering a solution).

- Webcam video recording (MS Window, Apple OS)
- Smartphone/tablet video recording (SocialCam, iOS, Android)
- Video and audio email (BombBomb, Talk Fusion, Jive Systems)
- Customer-generated content e.g., testimonials, video reviews (Bravo, Vidrack)
- Video distribution to multiple locations (OneLoad, Traffic Geyser)
- Video podcast hosting (Libsyn, Blubrry)
- Time-shifted video interviewing (Montage, Harqen, Take The Interview)
- Large file sharing (Hightail, WeTransfer)
- Screencast creation (Telestream, TechSmith)
- Video marketing feature add-ons (PressPlay, Easy Web Video)
- Syndication of video to a network of local websites
- Video integration with other applications (some of all of the above)

Most of these offerings have a monthly subscription price ($25 to hundreds of dollars per month) and they **all have unique user interfaces with various levels of complexity**.

No Good Options

Therefore, if a business wants to take full advantage of the marketing power of online video, **no good option exists.**

Sure, they could cobble together a solution consisting of a private video hosting system and multiple single-purpose apps — but, without the financial resources and technology staff to manage the complexity of a solution like this, it would **not be viable.**

In addition to the challenges with managing online video, there are **similar issues with managing online audio**. YouTube and most of the private video hosting systems are not an option. However, due to significantly smaller file size, audio files can often be uploaded directly to a website's server and played with the assistance of onsite plugin.

But, even so, single-purpose applications have been developed to meet the needs for online audio management (e.g., Audio Generator, Audio Acrobat) and audio podcast hosting (Libsyn, SoundCloud), which **creates another level of complexity**.

Then, beyond the complexities of managing video and audio, there is the **challenge of having to log into multiple accounts** (website, social media accounts, iTunes, etc.) to upload content. In response, services like HootSuite, SproutSocial and Shoutlet have been developed. However, they only enable text and image submissions (no video or audio) and they only distribute content to social media accounts (no website distribution).

This creates yet another level of complexity for the content marketer.

To summarize, to manage an effective content marketing effort using video, audio, text and image, you would need the following tools:

- Private video hosting system (video uploader, video converter, video player, but no video recorder)
- Selected (depending on your needs) single-purpose video apps
- Private audio hosting system (or embedded website solution for audio)
- Video and audio podcast hosting system
- Social media management tool

Again, it's certainly possible to manage a system like this, but it wouldn't be easy or affordable— and, as a result, it's **not being a viable option for the vast majority of businesses**.

Cold Calling

Does the very thought of cold calling make you shudder? You're not alone. Mastering the art of cold calling does take some practice, but with a little patience you'll soon be dialing your way to sales success.

The following tips can help you warm up to the idea of cold calling.

1. **Create a targeted list** – You wouldn't want to call apartment dwellers if you're selling roofing services. Having the right list of prospects saves you time and increase your chances of success.
2. **Organize and prioritize** – Now that you have your list, segment it into groups based on similar traits or specific needs. This will help you organize your approach and prioritize based on your goals.
3. **Be prepared** – The more you know, the more you sell. Take the time to research your prospects in advance so you can customize your pitch accordingly.
4. **Get social** – Use social media sites to research your prospects ahead of time. Then, if a call goes well, connect on LinkedIn so you can maintain contact and potentially connect with similar prospects.
5. **Understand your competition** – Find out who your competitors are, then research them thoroughly. Know what they're offering so you can point out what makes your product or service stand apart.
6. **Take the right approach** – Once you've researched your prospects, think about what you should say. Create a script as a guide, but do not read from it. Keep your tone friendly, confident, and enthusiastic.
7. **Take notes** – It's easy to forget important details when you're making lots of calls, so be sure to take copious

notes. Nothing is worse than not knowing what happened and then appearing to be disorganized or inattentive later on.

8. **Track your results** – Was the lead hot, cold, dead? As soon as you hang up, track your progress so you can start the conversation off on the right foot next time you call.

9. **Listen** – Don't dominate the conversation. After all, you want to get your prospect to open up about his/her needs so you can customize your pitch accordingly.

Finally, remember that cold calling shouldn't be your only marketing tool. Integrate email, direct mail, and search engine marketing into your overall plan—and drive your message home.

What's the easiest way to generate a leads list for cold calling?

It totally depends on the kind of leads you're generating. If you're generating B2B leads:-

Have someone (possibly an intern) create a list of companies and individuals, this may not include contact information.

Once you've the list ready, asks your person to find contact details by sending Linkedin request, searching on Google etc.

Send individual emails/linkedin messages and ask for a time and number for a call

Pick your best guy to make these calls. This is the moment when you've to make an impression.

Get a face-to-face meeting schedule. Go win the deal!

Exact Data

Exact Data provides multi-channel direct marketing services with a focus in database marketing lists and social media pay-per-click advertising. The company's database list offerings include postal mailing lists, 100% opt-in email marketing lists, and DNC-compliant telephone calling lists. Using the leading technology and comprehensive data hygiene and scoring process, Exact Data delivers the most accurate and continuously updated data available.

Exact Data, provides opt-in email lists for virtually any target market. All lists are 100% customize-able to fit your needs. Choose from business-to-consumer or business-to-business email leads. Filter by SIC Code, job title, interest, marital status, and more!

Exact Data is a direct-marketing firm specializing in multi-channel marketing services including postal, email, and telephone list solutions and targeted social media advertising. The Chicago-based company caters to businesses nationwide and services hundreds of thousands of clients ranging from SMBs to Fortune 500 companies.

The company was formed in 2001 and operates as a subsidiary of Exact Data LLC. With 100+ employees, the organization has been ranked on Inc. Magazine's 5000 fastest growing companies in America four years in a row and voted #1 for Data Card Quality by NextMark Inc. three years in a row.

Exact Data, a mailing list company headquartered in Chicago, IL, added new business-to-business international files to its database this week past week. These business-to-business marketing lists contain opt-in email addresses, postal addresses, and phone numbers for marketing towards globally-operating businesses and professionals working across the globe.

When targeting an international audience, narrowing the audience by geographical location is a primary way to enhance results by focusing on a specific country or region. Exact Data's international files contain high level decision makers and executives working in a variety of different industries throughout the world.

The company's business-to-business database is sortable by:

Geographic Location

SIC Code

Job Title

Job Function

and many other options

"Exact Data's new international files are the perfect resource for marketing professionals leading global campaigns," states Larry Organ, Exact Data CEO. "We are regularly adding new and valuable lists to our database, and these international files are no exception."

The company's records are consistently updated on a monthly basis, making them not only verified and accurate, but also highly deliverable.

Exact Data's updated international business-to-business markets include:

Australia International Business to Business Master File

China International Business to Business Master File

Mexico International Business to Business Master File

6 Tools Local Merchants Can Use to Grow Their Email Lists

Email marketing is cheap and it's effective, but it isn't always easy for small businesses. For local merchants, the toughest part about email marketing can be generating a list of engaged subscribers. According to a survey published by Ascend2 in 2015, 67% of businesses said growing their email list was "very important," and 43% said list growth expertise is the most challenging obstacle to success.

Email marketing vendors like Constant Contact and Mailchimp are introducing tools to make it easier for merchants to increase the size of their lists, and a number of new players have stepped in with products aimed at achieving this same goal. Here are six examples of tools that merchants can use to grow their email lists.

1. Cidewalk: Capture email leads via mobile advertisements.

Cidewalk integrates with Constant Contact to help businesses promote themselves locally and grow their email subscriber lists via mobile advertisements. Merchants create ads that appear as banners across the bottom of popular mobile apps in their local regions (like Pandora and The Weather Channel). Customers who are interested in those ads are prompted to email the merchant directly. With Cidewalk's new Constant Contact integration, which was announced in late 2015, these new email leads can be incorporated directly into Constant Contact workflows and added to prospect lists. Monthly subscriptions for Cidewalk start at $100 for up to 50,000 monthly impressions and two active promotions.

2. Wavelength: Find merchants with similar subscribers.

As a way to help its users grow their email lists more legitimately, the email marketing service MailChimp introduced an app called Wavelength in 2012. Wavelength allows MailChimp users to discover publishers like themselves and better understand their subscribers' other passions. Businesses can view sample emails sent by those other publishers, and they can use those samples as inspiration for their own email campaigns. More importantly, businesses can contact publishers with similar subscriber lists and link to each other—typically, with ads in each other's newsletters—for organic list growth. MailChimp offers free plans for businesses with up to 2,000 subscribers.

3. Exact Data: Purchase geo-targeted lists for email marketing campaigns.

Exact Data offers direct marketing services and provides businesses with email marketing solutions. Using the 242 million records in Exact Data's business-to-consumer database, brick-and-mortar merchants can build geo-targeted lists for their email marketing programs. These lists can be filtered by zip code, marketing channel, market type (business or consumer), demographics, and keywords. Exact Data says its lists are validated and run through a proprietary hygiene process prior to list turnover. Exact Data can also deploy email marketing campaigns from its whitelisted servers. Merchants can contact Exact Data for pricing information.

4. Square: Collect email addresses at the register.

In its ongoing effort to become a full-service shop for small business owners, Square added new email marketing tools to its platform last spring. Businesses can now capture customer contact information right from the register. Once the customer's contact information has been added, all information from subsequent visits—like purchase histories or transaction amounts—is automatically added to the business' customer directory. This data can then be used to target specific groups with email newsletters designed around their interests or spending habits. Square's tools for growing email subscriber lists are available for free.

5. iCapture: Let customers enter their own data at the POS.

Brick-and-mortar merchants can use iCapture to collect customer email addresses at the point-of-sale. iCapture turns any iPad, iPhone, or Android device into a tool for capturing leads. Businesses create their own forms with custom logos and fields using iCapture's Back Office software. They can then open iCapture's customer-facing app on whichever devices they're using in-store to let customers enter their own contact information. (Typically, this happens on a tablet displayed next to the register.) The captured data is retrievable at any time. Businesses also have the option to setup auto-reply emails or map their data to one of iCapture's integration partners. Pricing plans start at $10 per month, paid annually.

6. Privy: Take advantage of existing websites and social media pages.

Seventy-five percent of SMBs now have websites. Privy is a tool that helps businesses use their existing websites and social media accounts to grow their email lists. Privy uses a Javascript website widgets and mobile-friendly landing pages, combined with intelligent targeting, to encourage online visitors to share their email addresses. Geo-fencing tools are available to ensure businesses are only collecting email addresses from potential customers who live or work nearby. Local merchants can also use Privy's in-store offers to incentivize customers to join email lists and visit their brick-and-mortar stores. Privy offers a free plan for small businesses.

Yellow Pages

Simply fill out the form and your business profile will be listed at YP.ca for free (business name, address and phone number).

Why is it worth doing? Because Canadians searching YP.ca are looking to buy. So putting your business right where they're looking makes a lot of sense.

How many search YP.ca?

- 8+ million Canadians each month
- Plus, Canadians have downloaded the Yellow Pages app on smart phones 6+ million times

It takes less than a minute to fill out the form. So yes, it's worth it.

Search for local businesses by name to quickly find their Yellow Pages listings with basic details and maps, plus any additional time and money-saving features, such as coupons, video profiles or online reservations. Search by category to browse and filter local business listings and to see mapped results. Or, if you just have a number, search for a business by phone number to find its Yellow Pages listing just as well. Whatever method works for you best, it's all good.

The Yellow Pages online is the "traditional" phone directory Yellow Pages placed on the Web for easy access. This useful site offer residential and business listings, as well as maps, directions, and local attraction information. You can also create "collections" of useful links, as well as take advantage of local coupons.

The Yellow Pages online is the Web-based manifestation of the traditional Yellow Pages, which were originated in 1886 by Ruben Donnelly (see A History of the Yellow Pages).

The Yellow Pages online offers local listings, business directories, and free people search resources. YP.com focuses on United States listings exclusively, while Yellowpages.ca offers Canadian listings.

In addition to information directories and local listings, the Yellow Pages online also offers maps and driving directions, easily customized to include local gas stations, hotels, restaurants, etc.

How to find a business using the Yellow Pages:

Finding a business on the Yellow Pages online is quite streamlined: simply type in the name of the business you're looking for into the search box, as well as the city and state, and YP.com will return a list of results, usually geo-targeted at your specific location.

Results can be filtered by location, ratings, neighborhood, feature, etc. and also include maps, company websites, and phone numbers.

The Yellow Pages online offers a number of ways to find people for free in its listings, including:

By name: A last name is required in order to use this search. Results include name, address, and phone number (if available).

By phone number: Type in a phone number (including area code), and if the number is publicly accessible, a reverse lookup result will come back that includes the phone number, who it belongs to, and any applicable addresses (for more about reverse lookups, read Free Reverse Phone Lookup).

Address: A full street address, including city or zip code, is required.

Ads

Yellow Pages

Free Mobile Online

Online Business Directory

How to Look Up Address

People Search White Pages

Local Yellow Pages listings:

Local listings for major metropolitan areas include travel planning resources, local attractions, and popular categories ranging from plumbers to veterinarians (organized alphabetically).

Not Your Mama's Yellow Pages

We're all used to the standard big book of phone numbers dumped on our front porches, but as the Internet has evolved to become a bigger part of our lives than ever, that big book is becoming more and more obsolete. Using the Yellow Pages online to find what previously could take quite a bit of effort is an amazing timesaver.

Craigslist And Backpage

Backpage is a classified advertising website. It offers a wide variety of classified listings including automotive, jobs listings, real estate and services. Backpage is the second largest classified ad listing service on the Internet in the United States after Craigslist.

Near the turn of the 21st century, Internet-based classified advertising, particularly the website Craigslist, was having a significant impact on the classified advertising business in newspapers nationwide. Classified advertising in daily newspapers as well as weekly alternatives, suburban papers and community papers was moving to the free advertising model of Craigslist and other smaller websites. In 2004, in response to this phenomenon, New Times Media (later to be known as Village Voice Media), a publisher of 11 alternative newsweeklies, launched a free classified website called backpage.com. The foundation and traditions of free classified advertising and free circulation were part of the fundamentals of the alternative newsweeklies dating back to 1971. The Chicago Reader and the Phoenix New Times were pioneers in these operating philosophies.

Backpage soon became the second largest online classified site in the U.S. The site included all the various categories found in newspaper classified sections including those that were unique to and part of the First Amendment driven traditions of most alternative weeklies. These included personals (including adult-oriented personal ads), adult services, musicians and "New Age" services.

Craigslist vs Backpage for Marketing Your Services

Two places to market your services for free (or inexpensively) are Craigslist and Backpage. These classified ad sites are worth considering if you are just starting out and on a budget, but can still be effective for established businesses. Here is a quick comparison of the two services and the pros and cons.

Craigslist

Craigslist is the most popular classified ad site on the internet and whether people use it or not, most people know what it is. In most cities, you can post your ad for free, but some cities require a small fee to post.

Craigslist has a much wider user base than any other online classified ad site. So t the potential to reach more people this way is high.

Backpage

Backpage is a smaller site in terms of traffic, but some people say they get more business from it. (It gets about 3 million users a day versus craigslist's 64 million users per day.)

Backpage has a nicer design and cleaner interface.

Backpage has partnered with several newspapers. There are options to have your ad appear on newspaper websites, which can lead to higher quality traffic.

You will likely get less spam and scam replies from Backpage.

Most of the user base is in the U.S. (4 out of 5 people currently), so Backpage may not be as effective in other countries.

Both Sites

Here are some nice advantages of both sites.

Both sites are easy to sign up with and use.

Both sites are free or cheap to post ads.

In summary, try both sites out and see if each site is worth the time and effort for you and your business.

Big Media Advertising

Nothing gets the phone ringing and the orders coming in like lots of big media advertising. Newspapers, TV, and major Internet sites reach thousands, even millions, of potential customers around the clock.

TV advertising is very expensive. With prime-time 30-second commercials in medium-sized cities costing several thousand dollars each from companies looking to promote their new multi million-dollar product idea, broadcast TV ads are out of reach for most small and medium sized businesses. Mass appeal television lacks the ability to closely target the audience. Even if you can scrape together enough for a few TV commercials, much of your investment can be wasted on thousands of people who aren't interested in what you sell.

LOW COST AND TARGETED

Many media experts are recommending cable TV advertising to their clients. "Prime time spots on broadcast TV cost $2,000 to $3,000 in this area. Prime time cable spots go for $175," says Leslie Speidel, a media buyer in Raleigh, North Carolina (www.TheMarketingCoach.com).

Commercials on cable systems in the suburbs outside New York City are cheaper. Your 30 second spots run on CNN and ESPN for $25. Nick goes for $20 and TNN, BET, and VH-1 are $15 per commercial. Expect to get better rates when you buy packages of multiple spots.

Small town cable prices are even lower. It is not unusual to buy commercials for $2 to $3 in a town of 40,000 people.

While most of the commercials on cable TV programs are national spots for major corporations, four to six commercials per hour are made available to local advertisers. New digital technology allows many cable systems to easily and accurately schedule your commercials on specific channels to be seen in chosen communities and neighborhoods. "This new digital capability is great for placement purposes. The target is much focused. The geographic area is as big or as small as you want," Speidel points out. "Plus, the price of spots is affordable."

The ability to target specific groups of viewers is one of cable's most important advantages. A clothing store specializing in kids cloths can advertise on the Family Channel. A pool maintenance service can put their spots on the Weather Channel. In most cases, regular broadcast TV with more general programming would be inefficient advertising for specialized businesses like these. Take claims of big audiences with a grain of salt. It's not the number of eyeballs watching but a carefully targeted audience that gets results for your business.

PLACING YOUR ORDER AND PRODUCING YOUR COMMERCIAL

Cable rates, like everything in media, are highly negotiable. Some channels will cost more than others. The zones you choose to send your spots to, the size of your town, and the time of year will all have an influence on the spot price you pay. Don't wait until the last minute to place your spots. Plan weeks in advance. Placing your order early will ensure you get the times and channels you want at a lower price.

Call the sales department of your local cable operator. Find out spot rates and coverage areas. Take some time to build your plan. Media sales people are good at devising clever strategies to use your entire ad budget, so trust your own instincts and stay in control of the process.

Getting your commercial produced can be expensive and time consuming. A razzle-dazzle TV spot will easily cost thousands to produce. Keep costs down by planning your spot carefully. You won't want to make costly revisions while the production crew is there with the hourly meter ticking. Look into small one and two-person TV production services popping up in many cities.

Dramatic commercials with actors are best left to the networks. For a small business on a limited budget they rarely work out and often look amateurish. Keep your concept simple. Limit the number of locations. Budget time for changing lighting and mics from shot to shot. Shoot outside to avoid indoor lighting hassles.

How to Buy TV Advertising on a Budget: Why Buy TV Advertising

For certain types of small or mid-sized businesses, television may be a better advertising medium than any other. "Television is an attractive use of an advertising budget since it maximizes the reach of a commercial message and provides the opportunity for your potential customers to visually understand your service or product," says Lori Weston, a freelance media professional working in the Boston market with media buying service, Media Period, of West Bloomfield, Michigan.

If your product is visually appealing TV advertising may showcase that product better than other media, such as radio. "If you feel your product is better suited to people seeing it as opposed to hearing about it, then TV makes a lot of sense," Hroncich says.

What's more, television is "sexy," Weston says. "Television is captivating and holds an audience's attention," she says. "Additionally, if your ad fits in well with the programming where it's advertised, it could prove to be an outstanding tool in your marketing efforts."

Typically, an effective advertising campaign that includes TV advertising is expensive and complicated; however, it does not always need to be. With some patience, good negotiating skills, and an open mind you can buy TV on a budget.

How Much a TV Ad Will Cost

Before jumping in, you need to understand your budget for advertising. Be sure to include the costs associated with producing your commercial. You can produce your ad independently or with a television station, but costs can vary wildly. "It really depends on what you want," Hroncich says. "If you're a family-run business and you want to film a 30-second spot that shows a screen shot of your dinner special, it's not going to be very costly. But if there are actors employed, that will cost you more." He estimates that TV commercials can cost anywhere from $2,500 and up.

Then there is the cost of the advertising campaign. You typically don't want to spend your advertising budget all at once. You want to air it with a bit of frequency so that people will see it a number of times and it reaches a larger percentage of your target market. Typically, television stations will accept spot lengths of 10, 15, 30, and 60 seconds, and even longer if it is a direct response ad, Weston says.

You may have access to co-op advertising funds from manufacturers of products you sell that would augment your budget, Weston adds. "If so, make sure that you clearly understand the terms of qualifying for those funds, for example the ad may need to run a specific number of times or within a definitive time frame," she says.

How to Buy TV Advertising on a Budget: Target Your TV Ad Campaign

Before launching a TV ad campaign, you need to develop a plan for who you want to reach where, when, and how. Here are some considerations.

Geography. Options for advertising on TV include national networks, which reach a national audience; local broadcast or independent stations, which reach a regional or local market; and cable television, which can be national, regional, or local. "Any one or a combination of these can be used to achieve success," Weston says.

Target audience. Who is your core customer? "If you are trying to sell hearing aids your target audience would likely be adults 55 and older," Weston says. "Do not, under any circumstance, believe everyone is in your potential market."

Timing and seasonality. Identify any days or seasons that have the greatest potential for increased revenue, i.e. furniture stores target weekends and ski retailers target winter, Weston says. Something to keep in mind is that rates change every quarter -- broadcast TV rates usually rise in the fall when the new season starts for certain shows. Also, when a hotly contested election is on the horizon, demand for TV spots in certain markets may rise, Hroncich says.

How to Buy TV Ads on a Budget

Now that you know the basics, here are tips on how to find the bargains when it comes to advertising on TV.

Pay upfront. "Station sales representatives love this," Weston says. "They know the money is there, and their commissions are secured. They will work hard for you and maintain a schedule with little preemptions."

Commit to a multiple-week schedule. Most cost-efficient packages are sold on a 10-13 week basis, Weston says. "Stations much prefer to have spots booked ahead of time," she adds. "It helps them manage their inventory." If you work through a cable company that has many different stations, you might be able to strike up multiple week deals on a variety of programs. "If you are looking to advertise during the weekend, you could strike up a 13-week weekend schedule whereby your ad runs in live sports programming and news, along with old movies and syndicated programs," Weston says.

Take advantage of market conditions. If the local economy is slowing, chances are the airtime available on local television stations is aplenty and you can negotiate some terrific deals. That was the case during the recent economic downturn, when TV and cable companies were looking to fill their advertising slots and willing to negotiate.

Look for fire sales. "Although they don't happen very often, fire sales provide the opportunity to purchase advertising packages far in advance," Weston says. Quite often, they will include programming you would otherwise not be able to afford.

Auctions. When you purchase advertising via an auction, you will need to pay upfront, and may not have a clear understanding of what time slots you'll be receiving. Rather than base your entire television schedule on auctions, you may want to simply use the auction to complement your original schedule, Weston advises.

Buy remnant advertising. You can purchase inexpensive remnant packages with a range of flexibility; the more flexible you are, the more savings you will receive. "For example, you can purchase an 'auto-fill schedule' of 100 spots per week to air 6 a.m.-12 a.m., Monday through Friday," Weston says. "It may seem like a risky schedule, however at such a low cost if one or two spots air in a popular program this essentially 'pays' for the remaining spots."

Negotiate added value. When booking airtime, you can almost always negotiate for extras or "a value add," Hroncich says. "We did a cable TV buy for one of our clients recently and we got some free advertising on their website as a value add and some public service announcements at no charge." PSAs are 10-second spots to air when available during your flight (the schedule of advertising for a period of time). Hroncich says that advertising agencies can often help negotiate these value add deals better because they're aware of what the stations have offered other advertisers in the past.

Negotiate a media mix. Ask if the television station has a website and see if there are any potential promotional activities on that website if you buy TV advertising. "Negotiate to have your video commercial stream on a website," Weston says. "This is where TV trumps radio." While still advantageous, a radio ad streaming online does not carry the weight of a TV ad.

As you fine tune your TV advertising schedules, you'll start to realize the two or possibly three stations that provide the most value, Weston says. "If it is completely obvious, it's okay to drop the other stations considered," she says. "Develop a relationship with your best performers and invest in them. It will be worth your effort."

Fiveer

Fiverr is shaping the future of work, every day, by shifting the freelance economy online. Founded in 2010, with offices in New York City, Chicago, Miami, San Francisco and Tel Aviv, Fiverr is the world's most transacted marketplace for digital services. Its horizontal marketplace provides nearly any digital service in just one click, without haggling over the service deliverables or the price. Buyers can choose from the world's largest catalog of pre-packaged services ranging from graphic design to music/video editing to marketing and copywriting. Fiverr sellers looking to make extra cash have delivered millions of high-quality Gigs® from 150+ categories of services, and across 196 countries.

Fiveer provides social media marketing and management and virtual assistance to both local and global "solopreneurs," and small to medium-sized businesses, who want to build their networks and grow their presence on social media through release of relevant and engaging content, social customer service and social selling, and who need help with various virtual assistant tasks. Mission: To assist clients with social media optimization, social customer service and social selling, create engaging and entertaining content, and help increase brand awareness on various social media platforms.

FIVERR GIGS

Fiverr is a website wherein people who are skilled in their own way can generate income. This means that you can also be a part of the ever growing individuals who are making money with Fiverr.

Making money on Fiverr is easier than you think, at least in small quantities. There are a lot of opportunities for someone who knows how to do things, in fact anything can be monetized online.

Fiverr.com, is a website can help you make money by using your skills and where anyone can offer their services to anyone else for $5. Here's a few tips on how to effectively make money on Fiverr.

The main concept to this is you are to sell your services over at Fiverr and people who are interested about your services (services being offered are termed as "gigs") will eventually hire you and you will be paid $5 in each gig that you provide.

Take note that some services or gigs can be more than the $5 value but the main point of the system is to provide affordable services in which customers can surely pay for.

Well, $5 worth of your services is fair and unselfish enough since you can still earn more per gig.

This would only mean that you can earn more once you have multiple clients who are interested to your gigs. Be it about your skills or simply by selling your own physical products, you can still earn a hefty amount of money.

The good thing about Fiverr is that you can join anytime and it is free. This means that you don't have to pay for the websites services since it is also the way of the website to entice more and more people to join th'eir money making endeavors.

However, as for your information, you will only gain a profit of $4 in each gig you sell. The remaining $1 will be for the service payment method you will use (PayPal) and for the maintenance of the website.

This is to ensure that the website will generate more traffic through the efforts done by the owner and administrators of the website.

Now, as for the gig, you can create different gigs in which you think is "sellable". You need not worry about the kind of gig you can sell simply because you can sell just about anything.

Always remember that knowing your strengths in creating your gigs can be identified once you have started implementing it. In this way, you already have your own unique gig to offer at Fiverr and people who are interested in your "Fiverr masterpiece" will greatly reward you.

Moreover, you have to make sure that the gigs you have created using your skills should also be implemented within a time frame. This is to provide you and the client a better relationship.

If in the case you don't know when to start in creating your gigs, you can browse over at Fiverr and look search for relevant ideas in which you can use as your reference in creating your own gigs.

However, you have to make sure that your gigs are unique in a way that you don't have any competition over at Fiverr.

How to Post a Gig

First, you need to figure out which services you can offer. Perhaps you have a good voice and can offer to create short audio ads. Maybe you have a good appearance and want to provide video reviews about any products the buyer requires.

Many people go to Fiverr hoping to outsource some tasks related to their websites such as link building, webpage design, WP install, etc, for a very affordable price, of course because everything is sold for only 5 bucks!!

Not only website related products/services, but you can also find various different products/service since there is almost no limitation, just use your imagination, and if you find something that you think could attract people's interest then you can sell it there!

Adwords From Google

Location extensions show your business address, phone number, and other information (e.g. business hours and ratings) about your location.

On mobile, they can include buttons that allow customers to call or get directions to your business.

Clicks on ads with location extensions cost a standard cost-per-click.

How you benefit

Location extensions encourage people to visit you in person.

You can add multiple addresses by linking your account to Google My Business.

On average, ads with location extensions see a 10% boost in clickthrough rate.

You can target your ads around your business addresses.

Example

Zain owns a doughnut shop in Portland, and wants to draw foot traffic to his storefront. He adds a location extension to his ad. Now, people strolling around nearby who search for one of his keywords (like "best doughnut" or "doughnut shop") can see his address, a clickable "Call" button, and directions to his shop making it easier for potential customers to find him.

How your local business info can appear

What info can appear

Locations extensions can show the following information about your business address:

Business hours (including holiday hours)

Google reviews and ratings for your location

Phone number

Google will automatically pick the best information to be shown to users.

Where info can appear

Location extensions can show this information in various formats on the Google Search Network, Google Search Network Partner Sites, Google Maps, and on mobile devices.

Sites and devices where location extensions can show your business information (includes example ads)

How to set up location extensions

AdWords uses Google My Business to manage your business addresses.

Google My Business is a free service that helps customers finds you online.

It makes all your business addresses available for any campaign or ad group on the Search, Display, or Search with Display Select networks.

You can edit your business' hours (including special hours) with Google My Business.

You can use filters to control which addresses show up with your ads at the account, campaign, and ad group level.

Filtering options also let you choose whether a given campaign or ad group will show location extensions on all devices, desktop and tablet devices, or mobile phones only.

Blogging And Other Channels
To Get Yourself Out There

Blogging

Contribute guest posts to a well-known industry site: To find blogs to contribute to, do searches for "your niche" + "guest post".

Hold free webinars on your site: If you've investigated webinar software, you already know how costly they can be. Not to mention that most require a monthly subscription — not exactly small business-friendly! A great, low-cost alternative is using a WordPress webinar plugin like WebinarIgnition. It has a one-time cost of $97 for unlimited webinars with unlimited attendees.

Partner with a complementary business to co-sponsor a contest: Co-sponsoring the contest gives you access to each other's audience, maximizing your efforts. Submit your contest to popular sweepstakes sites to extend the reach of your contest.

Install a free social sharing plugin on your site: Using a free WordPress plugin like Share Buttons ensures all your blog content can be easily shared by your readers.

Comment thoughtfully on blogs in your niche: It's perfectly acceptable to leave your website URL in the appropriate field, just be sure to use your real name or business name, not keyword-rich anchor text.

Create an award for businesses or products in your niche: Create a simple badge using a free program like Canva, and then write a blog post of the Top 10 (e.g., Top 10 websites for Web designers). Award each of the winners with a badge that links back to the post. This strategy works best once your site has built up a reputation in your niche.

Other Channels to Get Yourself Out There

Join relevant industry forums and respond to questions with helpful advice: I'm not talking about writing spammy, thin comments just to gain links back your site. Make meaningful contributions to conversions to capture the attention of other readers.

Sign up with HARO (Help A Reporter Out) to get free PR for your business: Respond to relevant media queries and land free mentions and links in publications like Huffington Post, Forbes and other popular outlets.

Email a well-known business or influencer in your field with an authentic testimonial: Businesses love receiving testimonials, and many times will post them on their website (along with a link).

Invoice your business like a pro: Make sure that you're billing your clients on time each month as well as keeping track of everything. I personally love Due invoicing as it's a free option that invoices clients, and for a small fee you can bill people over PayPal.

Answer questions on a Q&A site like Quora: These sites consist of real people looking for answers to questions. Search the site for relevant questions you can answer intelligently.

Over To You…

The Internet has leveled the playing field significantly when it comes to marketing. The reach and visibility that used to only be available to big brands with big budgets are now within the reach of even the smallest businesses.

Importance of Digital Marketing

There's no denying it, the world is hastily transferring from analogue to digital. Human beings are consuming increasingly digital content material on a day by day basis – on cell phones, laptops, and more.

Commercial

Why is digital advertising so critical? Because it isn't only a unexpectedly developing force within the present day marketing gambling subject, it is set to be the destiny of advertising, and it appears probable that virtual media will soon update greater conventional paperwork altogether.

The facts are that virtual methods of verbal exchange and advertising and marketing are fast, versatile, realistic and streamlined. The best news is that digital gives just as a lot capability to marketers as it does to consumers.

Websites and seo content material

Blogs

Net banner advertisements

Online video content material

Pay-in line with-click on (%) advertising and marketing

E mail advertising and marketing

Social media advertising and marketing (fb, Twitter, LinkedIn, and so forth.)

Cell advertising and marketing (SMS, MMS, and so on.)

This is some distance from an exhaustive list, and new types of virtual advertising and marketing, inclusive of augmented fact, are arriving all of the time.

So, why virtual advertising?

Trending

How must meals producers approach exporting?

Confined Partnership or business enterprise?

Consumer engagement, demystified

To start with, digital advertising is infinitely lower priced than conventional offline marketing methods. An electronic mail or social media marketing campaign, for instance, can transmit a advertising and marketing message to clients for the merest fraction of the value of a television ad or print campaign, and potentially reach a much broader audience.

However, one of the major advantages of undertaking your advertising and marketing digitally is the ease with which results can be tracked and monitored. Instead of conducting costly consumer research, you may fast view customer reaction quotes and measure the success of your marketing campaign in real-time, enabling you to plot more correctly for the following one.

Conclusion

In today's times, customers have access to statistics at any time and at any vicinity. Small business owners, if they advertise and market right through social media, can ensure that their business will thrive and their customers will keep coming back for more, and with good reviews.

Why is digital advertising so vital to the business owner?

Because customers are relying more and more on digital channels to communicate with a business and to their friends and family. We are an instant society now. Posting comments about a business is a way of life now. Good reviews produce happy customers and attract new clients, as well as constructing a long-lasting relationship. However, be careful! It works both ways! Happy customers can help you, but an unhappy purchaser can damage your business instantly. Here are some ways you can work with social media to get positive reviews,

Encourage engagement thru virtual media

Have a fanpage and post interesting information. Invite your clients to follow you on twitter. These are a few suggestions and there are many others.

The more likes the higher!

Facebook likes and twitter followers and help your company grow in credibility. When a business owner uses these social media avenues to update customers about sales, events and other specials, their customers appreciate the attention.

Get to know your competition

Some companies spend large amounts of money on advertisements. Most small businesses cannot compete with them however, there is something they can do.

The Google alerts tool is a great way to monitor your competitors, and even your own business. This tool allows you to put alerts on certain key words or names to that every time that key word or name comes up in the industry or the news, you will be notified. It is important to keep up to date on what's going on with your competition.

Business recognition first!

The reputation of a business is essential. Without the agreement and self-assurance of the customer, a business would not continue to exist. If a business has a good reputation, clients will choose to stay. How to construct such an awesome reputation? Make sure you stay connected with your customers and anyone who interacts along with your organization through website, e-mail, and Social Media.

www.ingramcontent.com/pod-product-compliance
Lightning Source LLC
Chambersburg PA
CBHW060354190526
45169CB00002B/599